What's Inside?

Planes

A+

Smart Apple Media

Published by Smart Apple Media, an imprint of Black Rabbit Books
P.O. Box 3263, Mankato, Minnesota 56002
www.blackrabbitbooks.com

Produced by David West ☆☆ Children's Books
6 Princeton Court, 55 Felsham Road, London SW15 1AZ

Designed and illustrated by David West

Cataloging-in-Publication data is on file with the Library of Congress.
ISBN 978-1-62588-401-5
eBook ISBN 978-1-62588-431-2

Printed in China
CPSIA compliance information: DWCB16CP
010116

9 8 7 6 5 4 3 2 1

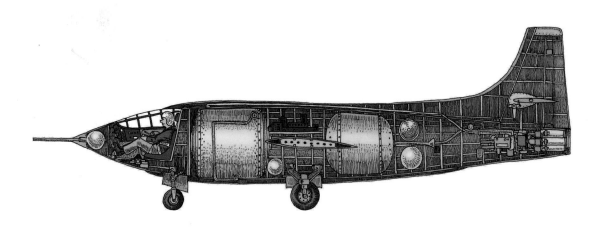

Contents

The First Planes

The first planes were covered in fabric. Most had two pairs of wings.

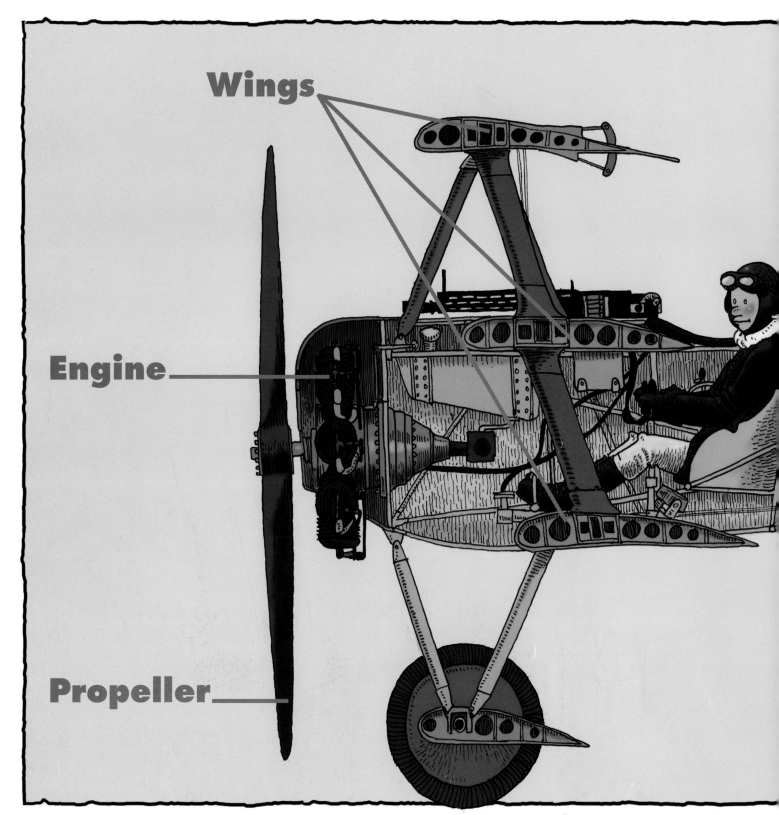

Wings

Engine

Propeller

Fokker Dr. 1

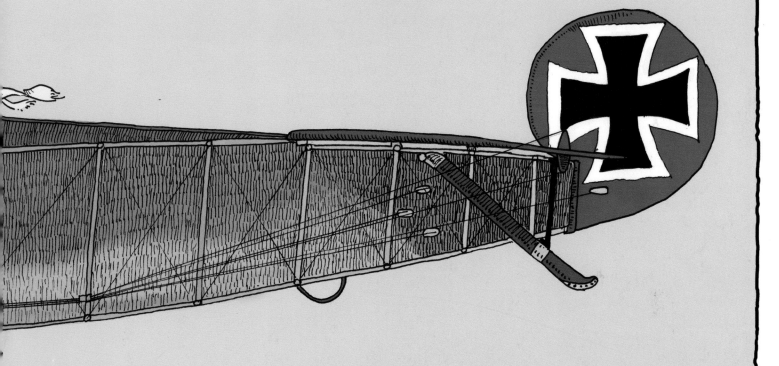

Flying Boats

Flying boats could land and take off on water. They could fly across oceans.

9

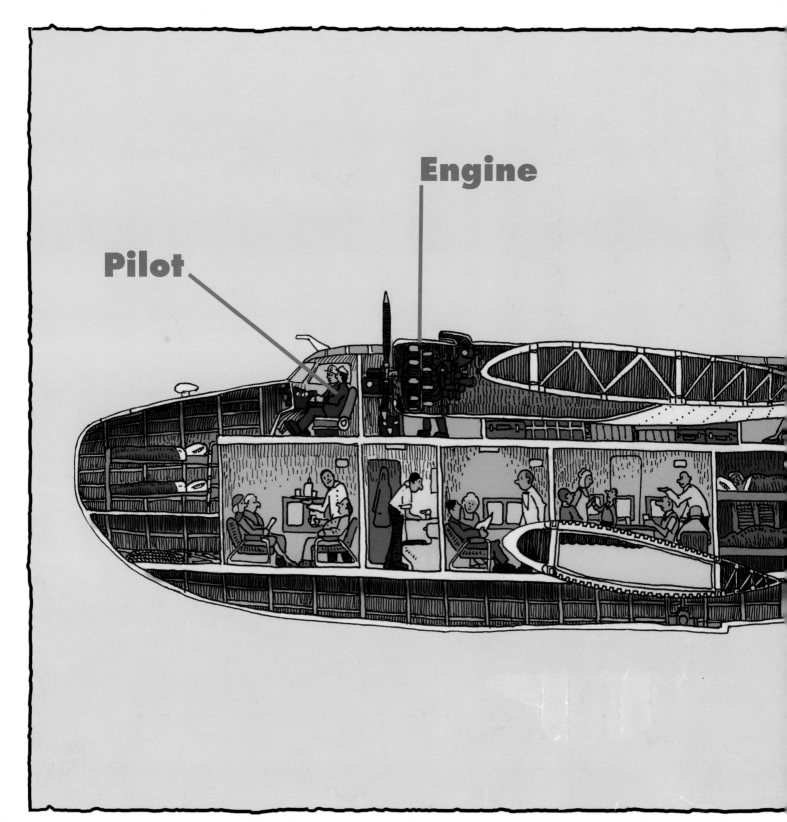

Boeing 314

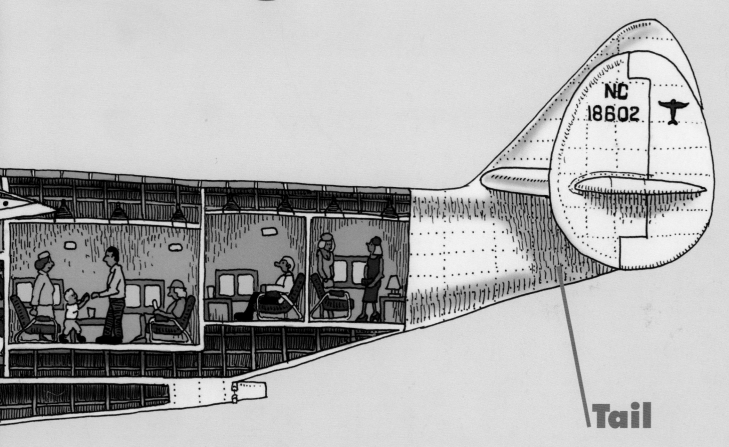

NC 18602

Tail

Bombers

Bombers have four or more engines. They carry bombs during war.

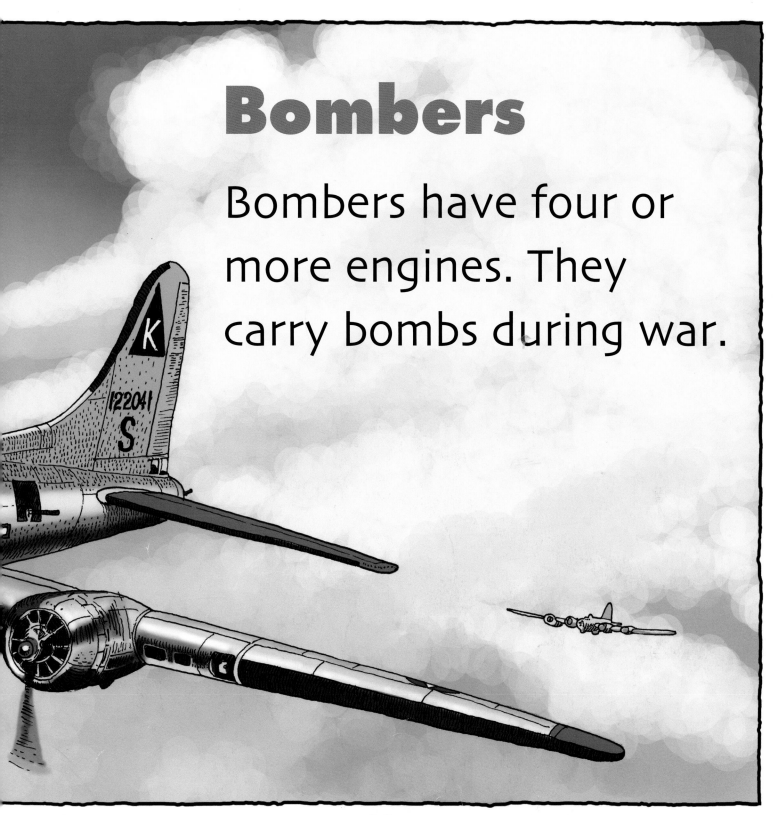

B-17 Flying Fortress

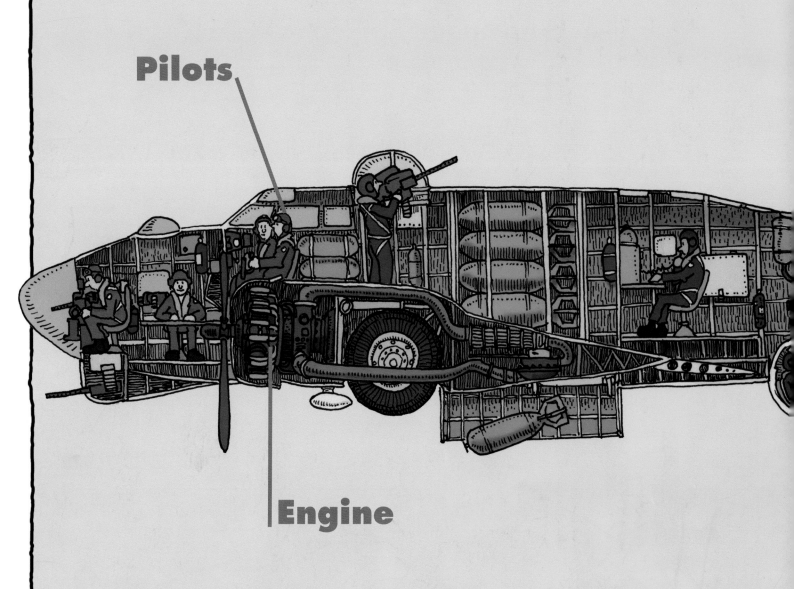

Pilots

Engine

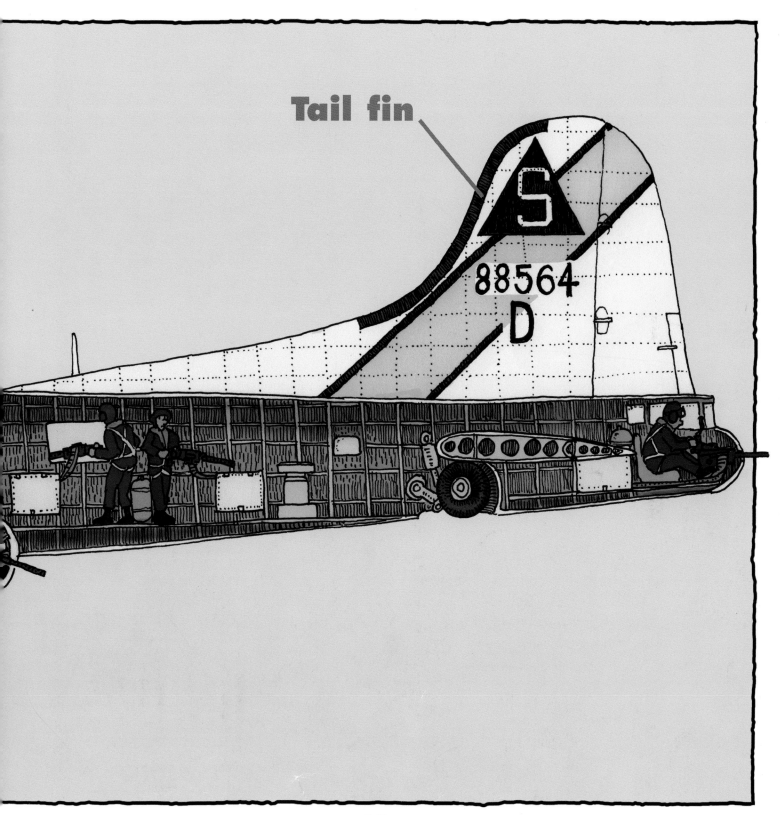

Tail fin

88564
D

Supersonic Planes

Supersonic planes are the fastest in the world. They go faster than the speed of sound.

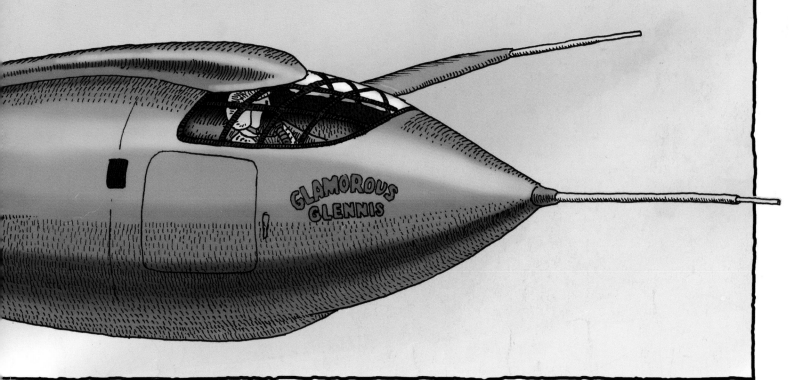

Bell X-1

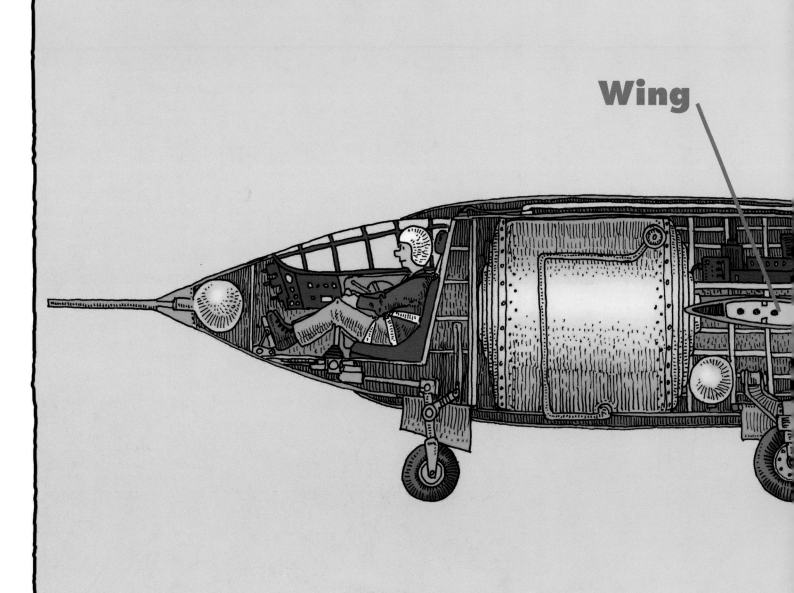

Wing

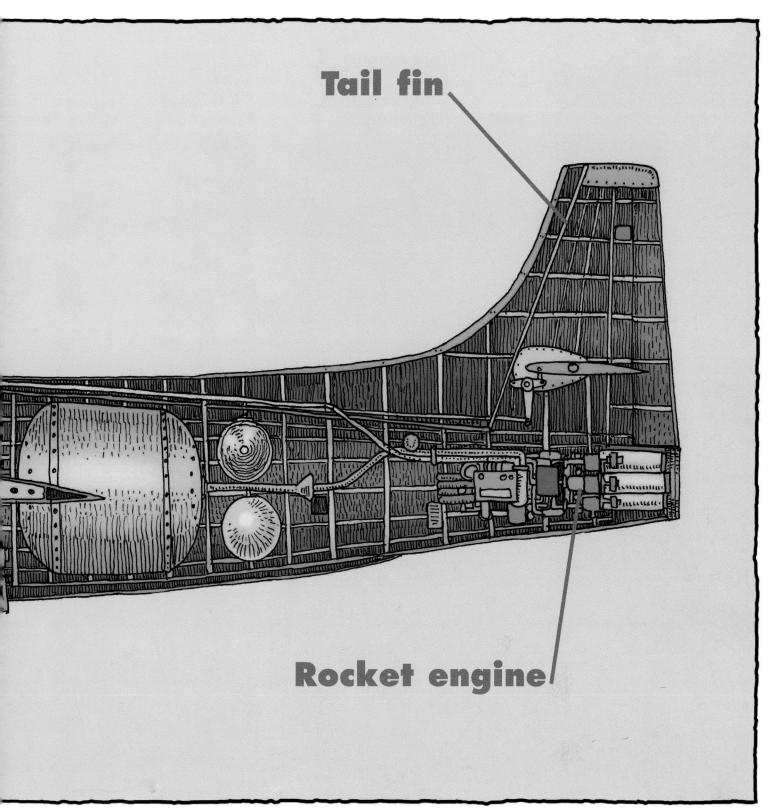

Tail fin

Rocket engine

Jet Airliners

Most people travel by jet airliners. Some airliners carry 850 people.

Falcon 8x

Wing

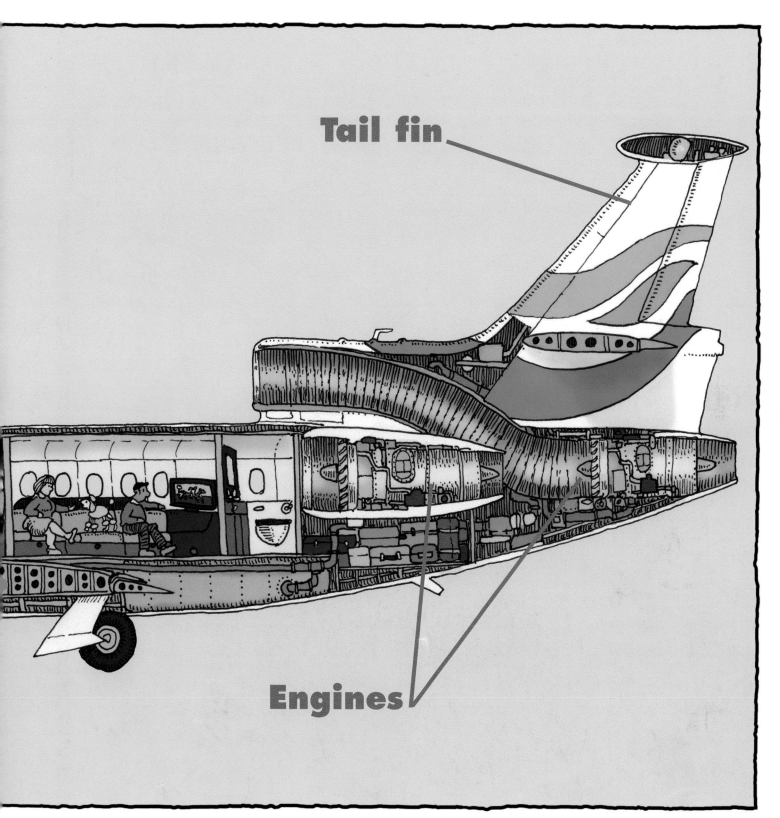

Tail fin

Engines

Glossary

engine

A machine that makes something move

pair

Two things that are the same and used together

fabric

A woven or knitted material

supersonic

Faster than the speed of sound, which is 761 mph (1,225 km/h)

Index